VIGILS

Sarah Akehurst

British Library Cataloguing in Publication Data:
a catalogue record for this publication
is available from the British Library

ISBN   978-1-912052-62-2

Typeset in 12pt Minion Pro at Haddington, Scotland

Printed by T J Books, Padstow

Cover designed by Baile Mòr Books

Contents

For Jonny – your book

Foreword

For over ten years, for one week each year, Jonny was my friend.

I too attended the camps that are referred to in the poems and sat round the bonfires that Jonny loved to build and poke and fan back into life the next morning.

Those camps were a place where many families gathered each year. Even though most of us didn't see each other for the other 51 weeks of the year, they created a bond and a companionship and a catalogue of shared memories that transcend the space and time within which those of us who have not yet died continue to travel.

Jonny is gone. And even though he was my friend for just that one week each year, his leaving has left a space that cannot be filled by anyone else, for he was, like me and you and everyone, a unique and particular person. The human ingredients that made him are a never to be repeated pattern. He was complete and lovely in himself. I remember and treasure his undefended, inquisitive and welcoming friendship. At the first camp I attended, when he could only have been about seven or eight years old, he was the first person to greet me; the first person to welcome me. He taught me how to make space for others.

These beautiful poems bring his memory back and also pierce the heart with the painful knowledge of a mother's love and the unimaginable sorrow of having to let go. In one of them – 'Christmas Day' – Sarah writes that "the hearts affection is a fire, the only fire whose brightness can illuminate the night."

I remember Jonny waiting for the campfire to be lit; and poking in its embers the next day, coaxing it back to life.

These poems do the same thing, prodding at the embers of memory and sorrow, joy and longing. Bringing them to life: "In the morning let me know your love, that is the only prayer I can manage now."

+Stephen Cottrell
Archbishop of York

Preface

This collection of poems is about my son Jonny. He died of cancer on 15th January 2020 and the poems are about my response to his illness and death.

The poems are ordered sequentially, covering a time period of about 18 months from November 2018 to May 2020. It may be helpful when reading them to have an idea of what was happening for Jonny, so I have written a brief account of this, which is at the end of the book. The poems also have dates.

'Vigils' is the name given to the office of night prayer, a very ancient monastic prayer time. It is prayer while waiting for the dawn, prayer which breaks up and sanctifies the night. And, of course, the word vigil has connotations of watchfulness, of staying awake and being with the ill or dying. Many of the pieces in the book were written at night when sleep was not possible, one on the last night of Jonny's life.

I would like to thank those friends and family members who gave critical attention to the poems in manuscript form, especially Jerry and Peter Akehurst, Mandy Nogarède-Perrons and Jude Edgar. I am very grateful to Olivia Macdonald for her sensitive illustrations, to Brian Thomas for his calligraphy, and to the Revd Jock Stein, editor of the Handsel Press, for all his assistance with the book.

Sarah Akehurst
February 2021

Sea Kayaking – November 2018

Even a single net of fish might be enough,
enough to feed a family, or sell,
working all night for nothing – empty nets
is a familiar feeling, nothing new.

But the miraculous catch of fish, imagine that -
more fish than anyone would want or need.
After the cold dawn, the flash of fish – enough
to break the nets and sink the boats,
silver, mysterious, quite new.
The fishermen, it says, were overcome.

You had a simple hope: to go
kayaking in the sea. In the mind's eye
I see the kayaks, bright as oilskins,
bright as dandelions, they weave
between the buoys and bigger boats,
between the seabirds perching on the rocks,
the rhythm of the paddle, the sea spray.

Someone said, *be careful, don't row out*
unless you know that you can row back home,
don't go too far. I think that you
have already drifted much too far –
between the drips and drains you float
out on the morphine tide,
awake you look accusingly at me,
I see no sign of any miracle.

8

It is November now, the darkest time,
the hospital is lost between the roads,
sirens on every side, and driving rain.
In early summer you set out, but now
the compass of the whirlpool draws you in.

I think of Mungo. This is where he lived,
close to a wooden church beside the burn,
a time of danger and of miracles,
dawn and dusk came quietly; he
kept vigil, prayed and worked and died.

I hope for what is ordinary,
what is enough; the miracle of
the tremendous catch which tore the nets
was not exactly what it seemed to be.
Might there be something, in the end,
better than what I hope for,
bright as sunlight, bright as miracles?

Radiotherapy – February 2019

Some things we shall never see
except by walking. Today,
between the icy showers,
I crossed a field to find
a way around the wooded hill,
then took a smaller path between the trees,
looking to shelter from the rain.

Kicking through last year's leaves
and over fallen trees,
the only sound the wind
and snapping twigs,
my footsteps muted by the forest floor.
This path leads nowhere, little used, ends
in what was once a quarry, years ago.

I find a wall of rock, damp,
dark with moss,
then unexpectedly in the dimness see
a flowering currant dancing,
fresh green leaves,
trailing cascades of blossom,
although it is the bleakest wintry day.

Often I have thought to take your hand
and go, walk further
than we have ever walked before –
walk to Alaska or Peru,
over the world's edge, anywhere
to get away from here.

This hospital, for all its cheerful paint,
is troubling, something implacable
brushes past us, bides its time and waits.
Before you leave there is a bell to ring,
but nothing tells us where this journey ends.
I'd rather walk forever if I could.

But just a little way away this dream of spring,
hidden, perhaps, from everyone
but me. Some things do disperse –
at least for now – the noonday demons:
singing, the shapes of stars,
the light of morning, and this plant,
flourishing and flowering in the gloom.
Some things we shall never see,
except by walking.

Today – April 2019

What did I do today?
Every part of life
seemed broken, splinters
and shards of glass,
nothing to hold on to.

This, a prayer to say
while kindling the fire,
to live this day, today,
without malice, envy, fear,
without terror of anyone
who goes under the sun,
only the Holy Son of God
to shield me, I say that to myself

and stay quiet
within the room, try to accept
with patience that this is how it is –
without malice, envy, fear,
without terror of anyone
who goes under the sun.

And walk under the sun, noticing
how the light falls on the white breasts of seagulls
sitting on every rock at many angles, how
the air is full of sounds, the sea sounds
and the bird calls, and the sand is strewn
with seaweed of many colours,
dotted with shells.

And here is something new –
sometimes words are found
which say the thing I want to say,
like a miraculous catch of fish –
a happy surprise after a long night
of catching nothing.

See Appendix 1

Picnic in July (Iona) – July 2019

How we sat on rocks among the shells, and it was raining,
you thought it was a good place, sheltered from the wind and rain.

How it was a place for shells, most broken,
deposited by high tides, caught in the gully.

How it was the most rudimentary of picnics –
a sandwich and two chocolate biscuits and an apple.
You did not eat the apple after all.

How I had thought a walk would help, walks have helped before,
it was a mistake that anyone might make,
apples too, many things have helped but can't help now.

How you looked at the shells and found two cowries,
and I found two little orange shells and a piece of purple sea urchin
and we put them in a limpet shell and brought them home.

How I used a bit of razor shell to stir my tea, and we agreed that if
you needed to have a knife then it would do for that as well.

How you weren't hungry and threw your sandwich to the seagulls.

How you said we could make rosaries out of shells,
though I could not quite see how.
And we looked at the shells and were puzzled, as we often are.

How you were too tired to walk, and slow.
How I knew that we might be done with picnics.
How we walked home slowly and I said that I'd better call the doctor.

How, later, when you'd gone, there were still the apple and the shells,
five of them inside a limpet shell, on the table.

How we never reached the beach we meant to go to,
just the beach in sight of home.

How when you'd gone I washed the flask and cups and went to work.
But later, when I knew you would not be back, looked at your room
and wondered if you would come back to it again.

Twenty years of picnics, well my dear, there will be picnics on my own,
and every one a time to think of you.

Picnic in July (Glasgow) – August 2019

I
If we started crying we might never stop.
If angels were to gather up these human tears,
even from an hour, they'd need
all the buckets I have ever owned –
even the children's buckets for the beach,
and every household vessel.
If they brought them to the throne of God,
presented them, would they dare to say,
really, are you sure?

It seems an unaccountable amount of tears,
the sufferings of those
with nothing much to lose,
who lost it anyway, who were not smart
or even sensible, who made the wrong decisions,
but still, so many tears, each pot brimful,
like the water jars at Cana. We're
not expecting any kind of miracle
or explanation, just asking
really, are you sure?

No angel would presume to ask,
what do we know? All there is to see
are these few shells, the gully on the beach,
your room, all your discarded things,
the usual objects, silence.

II
In the morning let me know your love,
that is the only prayer that I can manage now.
What does love look like –
like the light of morning,
like the bed of flowers
outside the hospital, all of the leaves
wet from the rain last night,
like your eyes?

In the morning let me know your love.
It isn't morning yet, not even light – this seems
to be the hardest kind of love
keeping vigil, waking in the dark,
remembering.

I will sing forever of your love O Lord –
maybe I will, although I think
most songs are silent.

III
Awake at night I listen to the trains
and hear the city birds who greet the dawn,
although I never see them in the day.
And what has brought such sorrow to my heart
is not your dying but the life you had,
grafted to the wood that made the cross,
twenty years of living, unconsoled.

And the love I bear Our Lady and the Lord
is not separate from your life, nor separate from
the sadness of the world through which we walk,
here, where Mungo lived beside the burn,
and where he met Columba by the well,
singing psalms, the same psalms we sing still.

I only see the rain, the surfaces,
and do not know the place where the light dwells,
nor see the gate of death, nor understand
which seeds are watered by our tears, and grow.

Bay at the Back of the Ocean –
September 2019

I

Now is the time of storms,
I watch the forecast, think
if we were home, we'd walk
across the machair to the sea,
there'd be a kind of silence filled
with sound, gusts of wind and
water tumbling stones.

Shades of seaweed gleam
in shafts of sunlight all around the stones,
rose-pink and grey, (some shaped like hearts),
many colours, many kinds of stones,
the storm clouds and the silver sea,
squalls and blue spaces in between.

II

In the city so few words were said:
you would not recover, there were
only weeks or, with the treatment,
months. Did we have questions?
Out in the bay, the breaking waves
show where the rocks are when the tide is high.
We had no questions, had no words at all.

A smiling doctor said you'd lose your hair,
and when you did, we stood
outside the barbers shop and were
the quietest people on the city street.
The doctor said it might grow back
after a year; we knew
you did not have a year.

The stairwell at the hospital
has posters on the walls, they say
if every day you climb the stairs, then soon
you will have climbed a mountain;
eventually you might have climbed
them all. We look at photographs
of Scottish mountains on the walls.

You can't climb mountains now,
with just one lung, nor stairs;
we take the lift, you with the drip stand
and the bag of drugs. I think about
the island hills in autumn –
only the sound of wind, the sound
of water running over stones. I think
there is no need to suffer well.

III
One day a gift came in the post,
a model, something complex to construct;
the best of gifts, it only needs one hand.
You pace yourself, because it needs to last –
immersed, methodical, and still
tenacious of life, not in a grasping way;
you simply want to live.

I piece the days together,
bright mornings, bitter times,
injections, clinics, side effects.
Leaves blow along the pavements
as the nights close in. I pray,
if we're not strong enough
to walk this road, please do it for us,
do it with us, and every night I
lie awake and listen.

IV
"Do not let your hearts be troubled.
In my Father's house are many rooms
many, many rooms, a room for you."
For now, it's dark, too dark to see
any houses, any kind of rooms, only
Our Lady of the Sea, I think of her.

Now is the time of storms, the spray
flung from the spouting cave is
blown above the waves toward the shore.
It shimmers and dissolves into the air,
moving with the wind as if it were
an unknown element, as if it were
a different kind of light.

When I no longer see you,
when you've gone,
I'll watch the spray and walk
between the tumbled stones,
(some shaped like hearts).
Today I keep the vigil, ask
Our Lady of the Sea to stay with us,
in the hour of death, and also now.

Many, many rooms, a room for you,
but I don't see it here, this room for you,
only the silence and the news of storms,
far from morning, far away from home,
the seaweed glimmer on the shore,
all of the colours, all the shapes of stones.

Christmas Day – December 2019

On Christmas Day you stumbled, almost fell,
said you could go no further.
I said *you're nearly there, it's not far now.*
No angel voices as you staggered home.
I think Christ's mother always knew
what suffering was like, and knew
the heart's affection is a fire, the only fire
whose brightness can illuminate the night.

Burns and scars, the treatment didn't work,
though we lit candles, asked the saints
to intercede for you. One last novena,
through to Christmas Eve,
paying out the nets just one more time
so not to miss a miracle – who knows?
I'd prayed for help from someone
quite like you, young with a ready smile.
The saints stay close to us, they understand.

No miracle of healing even so,
only the road diverging. The child
who came so ardently to earth
recoiled from drinking such a bitter cup –
each joyful mystery becomes
a mystery of helplessness and trust,
one draught for you to drink,
one path, not far to go.

After the Rain – January 2020

"I am distressed for you, my brother Jonathan" – 2 Samuel 1: 26

After the rain, the park seems stunned,
as if the weight of water all night long
has brought it down to silence;
though by the time I reach the bridge,
the first dogs venture out,
then joggers, dodging pools,
call to each other. The sun
touches branches, garlanded with raindrops
bright as diamonds, bright as miracles.

I am distressed for you, for you
will not be part of this, will never
walk a dog, or run, this crowded city
holds no place for you. Sojourners,
we pitched our tent and lived
like wraiths beside the river in the park.

Going to the hospital, that's all
we did for long enough, the park,
the bus. Today, from the upper deck
I see far in the West are hills,
lit by a burst of January sun
after the weeks of rain, and
the distress I feel for you wells up –
all the heroic walks you planned
to help the cancer charities.

The hills dissolve, recede, here is
the hospital stop.

Tonight, I share your room and hope
that we might sleep, that you might not
call out all night, that this might not be,
after all, a night to die,
though if it's not tonight, it will be soon.
And nothing will have changed,
the city and the rain, the distant hills,
the magpies with the nest outside your window.
You cry, I am distressed for you, for you
were lovely in life and comely, full of hope.

I imagine nothing beyond this night –
a place to suffer and a place to wait –
and the way to heaven, I don't know
how you would get there – if the park,
the river and the bus might be a way?
After your hair grew back,
you seemed both more familiar
and changed. How will you look to me
when you have gone?

Did you agree to this, agree to be
grafted to the wood that made the Cross?
Twenty-one years since you were born,
tonight I think I've had enough of deals,
hope and distress twine with the tangled sheets,
here you will leave us – Mungo's city,
Mungo's dear green place,
where he stayed to comfort the forlorn –
and pray, may he pray now for us
until day breaks and all the shadows flee.

Remembering – May 2020

Remember the picnic in July?
I made a rosary from shells,
you have to use the broken ones,
it wasn't such a puzzle after all.
Your father wondered what it was, he said,
"You'll never make a living out of that."

Well, none of our ideas would make us rich,
we were beginners; it turned out
you need not make a living after all,
that cross was lifted from you.
Those who spin straw to gold,
can keep their secrets, alchemy
was not required of you.

I keep on making things from other things –
from what's discarded,
that is how I best remember you.
And you did not keep anything –
after you took your hand out of the fire,
you smiled and then gave everything away.

Someone saw a magpie, near our home
the first for years. There are no kayaks now,
only the quiet sea where dolphins play,
the heron flying from the gully, this is
a time for mourning, spring
turns to summer imperceptibly.

Here where we picnicked in July,
here we walked the very last time home
before you ran ahead,
flying like sparks through stubble,
before you shone as gold
tried in the furnace,
an offering accepted, though
we had no thought of that.

I walk to all the places where we went,
then home,
with pockets full of shells,
still spinning straw to other kinds of straw,
remembering
we are only ever dust,
though clothed in mercy,
always beginning,
thinking still of you.

Jonathan – 15th July 2020

Not to forget the smallest thing –
your dark head on the pillows,
how you called out, your head was sore,
calling for water, morphine, for a nurse,
a book, why did you want a book?
You rarely read a book.

You rarely read a book.
I used to tell you stories about mice.
I could have made one up to tell to you
through the long restless night,
before that last slow breath;
now half a year has passed.

Half a year has passed, and you
stay quiet, well, you were always quiet.
Now and then I find a heart-shaped stone
and wonder if it is a gift from you.
When you were born you were yourself a gift,
though not a gift to keep – it's hard
to look at photographs of you.

You in a photograph. Today
I found one taken long ago –
the camp, it was our holiday each year;
you sit beside a massive pile of wood,

your brother and his friends have work to do,
they hardly notice you, but there you sit,
although the bonfire won't be lit for hours.

The bonfire won't be lit for hours,
but you are ready on your camping stool,
you look alone and frail, that's how it was,
wearing a blue sweatshirt with a hood, there is
an expression of great sweetness on your face.

An expression of great sweetness on your face,
wearing a blue sweatshirt with a hood,
and crying out all night your head was sore,
for water, for a nurse and for a book.
I only want to go to heaven if you're there,
and if your arm is mended, and your hand,
if you can make things, if it's ordinary.

Ordinary with things to make,
and kayaks, stories, ordinary things,
and, if the fire is lit at dusk and we
can bring our camping chairs and sit,
watch as showers of sparks fly up and
if the brightest flames show me
your face. For now there's silence,
milestones, memory, I hope
never to forget the smallest thing.

Jonny's story

Jonny was born with a genetic condition, Neurofibromatosis Type 1 (Nf1). This caused him a range of difficulties as he was growing up, including difficulties with learning; life was never easy for him. Jonny had a passion for music and guitar making, and after leaving school he started a course learning how to make stringed instruments. He spent six months doing this in Glasgow before having to stop because of the cancer. He was never able to go back to the course, although always hoped to. Having Nf1 was the reason why Jonny developed a rare type of cancer, a malignant nerve-sheath tumour.

All cancer journeys differ, but many include some of the same elements. For Jonny the journey started with his going to the GP in July 2018 because he had a lump in his upper arm. He first mentioned this because he was finding he could not properly use his left hand and it was becoming difficult to play instruments or use tools. The tumour was the reason for this, as it was pressing on a nerve. The lump turned out to be malignant and he had a lengthy and complex operation in Glasgow to remove it in November. Afterwards he could not use his left hand and had very little strength in his arm.

Jonny had radiotherapy in Glasgow from January to March 2019. Surgery to try and restore lost function in his arm and hand was due in July 2019, but just before that he became very ill, and it was found that the cancer had spread to the cavity of his lung. This was a turning point, because after this we knew he would not survive – there had always been some hope before then, though the cancer he had was very aggressive.

Instead of the planned surgery, Jonny went first to Oban hospital then back to Glasgow. He then had chemotherapy for four months in Glasgow, with the aim of giving him longer to live and a better quality of life.

After this ended, Jonny had about a month at home in Iona in November before there were signs that the cancer was active again. By Christmas Day he was having new and troubling symptoms, which turned out to be caused by a brain tumour. Jonny was admitted to the Beatson West of Scotland Cancer Centre in Glasgow on December 30th, the day after his 21st birthday, and stayed there until he died on 15th January 2020.

The poems were nearly all written in Iona or Glasgow. Over the time of Jonny's illness he and I spent months in Glasgow as he had to stay there for treatment at the Beatson.

Jonny suffered a great deal, but he rarely complained. He kept his smile and his sense of humour – rather dark at times – and enjoyed life as far as he could, right up until the end.

Appendix 1

Blessing from *Carmina Gaedelica* referred to in the poem 'Today'

I will kindle my fire this morning
In the presence of the holy angels of heaven,
In the presence of Ariel of the loveliest form,
In the presence of Uriel of the myriad charms,
Without malice, without envy, without jealousy,
Without fear, without terror of anyone under the sun,
But the Holy Son of God to shield me;
Without malice, without envy, without jealousy,
Without fear, without terror of anyone under the sun,
But the Holy Son of God to shield me.

God, kindle Thou in my heart within
A flame of love to my neighbour,
To my friend, to my foe, to my kindred all;
To the brave, to the knave, to the thrall;
O Son of the loveliest Mary,
From the lowliest thing that liveth
To the Name that is highest of all.
O Son of the loveliest Mary,
From the lowliest thing that liveth
To the Name that is highest of all.

Appendix 2

It may be useful to have some information about the people and ideas referred to in the poems.

St Mungo (also known by his birth name of Kentigern), is the 6th-century patron saint of Glasgow. St Columba came from Ireland to Iona, where we live, also in the 6th century. They are thought to have met at a well near to where Mungo lived, now known as St Mungo's well. Mungo lived close to where Glasgow Royal Infirmary has been built, and he is buried in the crypt of Glasgow Cathedral, which is next to the hospital. Jonny had his operation in this hospital. Mungo is referred to in 'Sea Kayaking', 'Picnic in July (Glasgow)' and 'After the Rain'. Columba is referred to in 'Picnic in July (Glasgow)'.

There is a reference in 'Christmas Day' to "someone quite like you" – this is the Venerable Margaret Sinclair, who died in 1925 aged 25. She grew up in a tenement flat in Edinburgh, and left school to start work when she was 14. She was known for being hard working, cheerful, and kind, someone to whom ordinary people could relate. Pope John Paul II said that "Margaret could well be described as one of God's little ones, who through her very simplicity, was touched by God with the strength of real holiness of life."

The references in 'Remembering' to "beginners" and "beginning" allude to the Rule of St Benedict, written in the 6th century as a guide for his community. St Benedict describes it as "a little rule for beginners".

Several of the poems refer, directly or indirectly, to the writings of Saint Thérèse of Lisieux. Thérèse's writings and her example underpin much of what is in this book. Thérèse's relics came to St Andrew's Roman Catholic Cathedral in Glasgow in September 2019 whilst we were there, and many people prayed for her intercession for Jonny in the hope that he would be cured, though this was not to be.

Thérèse herself died of tuberculosis at the age of 24, after much suffering. She did not look for any tangible consolation from her faith, but tried to accept what was given to her as lovingly as possible, not seeking anything easier or harder. She wrote that there was no need to suffer well or to make a success of suffering. She believed that every Christian is given a share of the cross to carry, and that the mystery of the cross can be lived out in the most ordinary and everyday encounters and trials of life. It is a mystery of helplessness and trust, "not a mystery of bravery, but a mystery of love".*

* Bernard Bro (1979) *The Little Way – The Spirituality of Thérèse of Lisieux.*

Also by Sarah Akehurst:

In Firmamento Caeli

An illustrated book of poems about hope, published in 2019, written out of Sarah's experience of being a companion to two people with different disabling and incurable conditions. Many of the poems are set in Iona or Pluscarden Abbey in Morayshire.

available from the author at sarahakehurst7@gmail.com

Check out the *Sanctus Media Handsel Press Bookstore* for other poetry booklets . . .